MEMORABILIA
OF THE CIVIL WAR

William C. Davis

Designed by Philip Clucas

Featuring the Photography of Tria Giovan

MALLARD PRESS
An imprint of BDD Promotional Book Company, Inc.,
666 Fifth Avenue, New York, N.Y. 10103.
Mallard Press and its accompanying design and logo are trademarks of
BDD Promotional Book Company, Inc.
CLB 2738
© 1991 Colour Library Books Ltd., Godalming, Surrey, England.
First published in the United States of America 1991 by The Mallard Press.
Printed and bound in Singapore by Kim Hup Lee.
All rights reserved
ISBN 0 792 5558 4

MALLARD
PRESS

INTRODUCTION

Johnny Reb and Billy Yank had very few possessions. For an infantryman, or even a cavalryman or artilleryman, it did not pay to acquire much, because whatever he owned he had to carry with him. Very few Civil War soldiers took up rock collecting! The few who were literate rarely carried more than one book with them. Souvenirs and personal items not vital to his day-to-day life, the foot soldier of 1861-1865 simply left behind. Everything that mattered to him had to be bundled up, either on his person or in his knapsack, and carried from dawn to dusk, from bivouac to bivouac. His was a small world of few belongings, and all his worldly belongings had to travel with him.

FACING PAGE: When Johnny Reb and Billy Yank went to war, they went as simple folk, with simple needs.

CHAPTER ONE

UNIFORMS

The private soldier consisted of one man," wrote an old veteran, "one hat, one jacket, one shirt, one pair of pants, one pair of drawers, one pair of shoes and one pair of socks." That was not far off the mark. Setting aside his weapon, a soldier almost literally was his uniform.

Certainly that was how the people of the era saw soldiers. Theirs was a time just at the end of a centuries-long era when people expected soldiers to be almost gaudily colorful. Especially after the flamboyance of the Napoleonic era, the armies of the world designed their uniforms more for parade show than utility or comfort.

The American Civil War, in fact a modern war in

ABOVE: The war's first uniforms came from militia units like Charleston, South Carolina's Washington Light Infantry.
FACING PAGE: the 33d New Jersey.

so many ways, also presaged the dramatic shift from individuality to uniformity in military dress. The so-called "Old Army" of the United States before the war paved the way, with a basic enlisted men's and officers' dress that was much understated compared to European counterparts. Americans dressed in simple blue, with little ornamentation on regulation dress other than brass buttons and colored trouser stripes, and jacket insignia denoting rank and branch of service.

When the war came in 1861, both North and South attempted to follow the same basic pattern. Regulations in the Union called for sky blue trousers,

with a yellow stripe for cavalry, red for artillery, and blue for infantry. The jacket or blouse was to be dark blue wool, tapered to the waist, with a slight "skirt" below reaching about halfway to the knee, though regulations later allowed a shorter "sack" coat that extended only a few inches below the waist. Insignia of rank – sleeve chevrons for non-commissioned officers, bullion-fringed shoulder straps for officers – were to be in the color corresponding to the branch of service.

RIGHT: The wonderful colorfulness of Civil War uniforms is evident in these Zouave trousers and shell jackets. The hats include the French kepi and Algerian fez. Natty canvas leggings, sashes, and elaborate "frogging" on the the jackets complete the festive attire.

The greatest variety came in the headgear. Regulations provided that enlisted men wear the Hardee, or "Jeff Davis" hat, a dark, high-crowned affair with a wide brim, turned up on the left side for infantry, and on the right for other branches. Officers in the Regular Army were to wear this, too, but quickly other variations appeared. Nothing was more individual to a man that his hat, and so it was in the army. The French style "kepi," a close cloth hat tapering upward from the bottom to a round

ABOVE: Headgear alone offered a bewildering variety of shapes and colors. Top right is a fairly standard kepi from the 129th New York. A Zouave fez is beneath it, and to the bottom left is the forage cap, little liked by anyone. Top left is a very colorful, full red kepi, probably from a New York Zouave regiment.

RIGHT: A standard regulation Confederate kepi of light blue fabric with a black leather visor. The brass letter on the front denotes the solder's company.
FACING PAGE: Men of the 9th Indiana Infantry, posing somewhere in Tennessee. A variety of uniform elements are in evidence, from the short shell jacket usually worn by cavalrymen and artillerymen, to the standard sack coat. These so-called Western regiments were notoriously informal about their adherence to uniform regulations, their eyes set always on utility and comfort.

BELOW: Confederates always presented the greatest variety of all, as shown by these Rebs on Morris Island, South Carolina, in the days just after the firing on Fort Sumter. There is not a single genuine, complete uniform among them.

shape with a flat top, with a simple leather visor in front, soon became ubiquitous. It did little for the soldier other than keep the sun from his eyes at noonday, but it was simple and easy to make. Havelocks, cloth coverings for the kepi that draped down behind to cover the neck on sunny days, were quickly discarded by the men, who found them hot and uncomfortable, and more useful as dishrags and coffee strainers. The most extreme development was the forage cap, literally a kepi gone wrong, the tapered top extended forward, accordion-like, until it drooped above the visor and looked like the bulbous snout of a seal elephant.

When they could get away with it, many Yankees, especially from west of the Alleghenies, discarded kepis and forage caps alike, and opted for "a good soft felt hat," as one said.

Their Confederate counterparts were even more individualistic. Southern regulations provided only for the kepi, but with the constant scarcity of supply, most soldiers wore whatever they could get

or bring from home, from shapeless "slouch" hats, to straw Panama's, and even huge Texas sombreros. It was the same with the rest of Johnny Reb's uniform. Regulations were honored mostly in the breach, thanks to scarce supply. The ideal soldier was to wear trousers and long blouse of "cadet" or "Confederate" gray, with trim virtually the same as with the Union services. In practice, homemade dyes had to be used, and most often the cloth came out a kind of "butternut" brown. Cavalrymen and artillerymen in both armies were supposed to wear

FACING PAGE: The vivid color and variety to be found in uniforms of some of the Union regiments, including a highland kilt, knee stockings, and the flared jacket and sporran, and feathered hat of the 79th New York Highlanders. ABOVE: The ideal uniforms of Union (left) and Confederate (right) soldiers were not often achieved.

A further confusion in uniforms came about when regiments used the other side's colors, as with this gray coatee from a Union militia outfit.

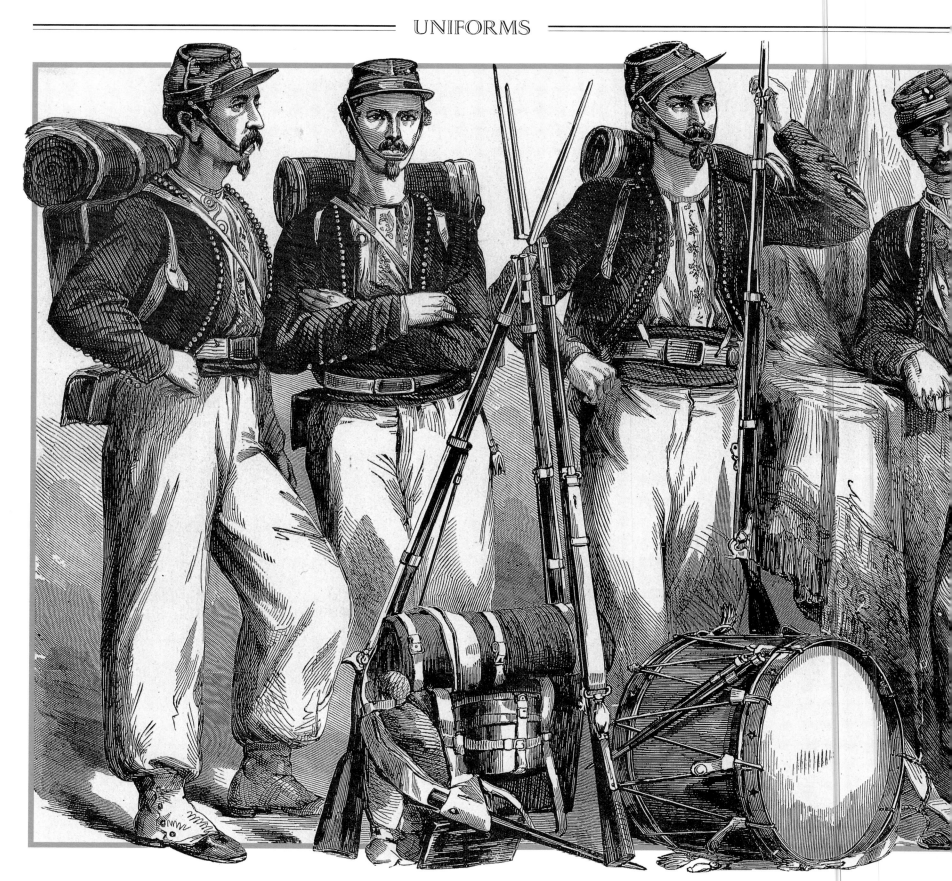

FACING PAGE: One of the war's first and most famous unusual units was the Chicago Zouave Cadets, raised by President Lincoln's friend E. Elmer Ellsworth, who would be the first Union officer killed in the war. LEFT: An early war Federal dressed in gray, Lieutenant Henry Richardson of the 21st Massachusetts displays a swallow-tailed coatee, frogging, and more.

ABOVE: Colonel Abram Duryea commanded another famed Zouave regiment, and would lose his life during the war. There was almost a comic-opera aspect to some of the gaudy trappings of the Zouaves, but it did nothing to impair them as soldiers.

a shorter "shell" jacket, rather close fitting and extending only to the waist. It was also intended that soldiers of all branches were to be issued with an overcoat or "greatcoat," single-breasted like their tunics. In the Union army they usually got them, but they did not keep them for long. The heavy wool coats were cumbersome and uncomfortable, even in cold weather, and many if not most soldiers eventually sold or traded them away, or just left them by a roadside. Confederates simply never got them.

Underwear, really just long "drawers," was cotton or flannel, and socks generally wool, but soldiers went through such garments quickly, and supply never kept up with demand. Indeed, the average

ABOVE: A fanciful 1861 lithograph depicting the First Battle of Manassas, or Bull Run, shows the preoccupation of the public mind with the Zouaves, in the right foreground, and the natty regulars in their havelocks at left. The mounted Confederate cavalrymen, too, look resplendent in their frogged jackets. **RIGHT:** A sketch showing a variety of Confederate uniforms: artilleryman at left, infantry general next to him, cavalry general in the center, mounted and dismounted cavalrymen next, and an infantryman on the far right. **FACING PAGE:** A Yankee cavalryman's shell jacket and bugle.

soldier Blue and Gray was none too fastidious about his dress, or about caring for it, with the result that most such items did not survive the war. Even the uniform jackets and trousers that did survive were usually in bad repair, and often altered to suit some soldier's individual taste or flair, especially in the Confederate army, where many men never got a regulation uniform to start with, and virtually chose their own "military" dress.

As if short supply and individuality were not enough of a hindrance to efficiency, there were literally hundreds of state, local, and private outfits that never even attempted to adhere to the national regulations. When the war first erupted, scores of state and local militia units that already existed were quickly volunteered for national service. They came with their pre-war weapons and uniforms in a rainbow of colors. The 7th New York State Militia

arrived in beautiful gray, while outfits like Virginia's Lynchburg Rifles came attired in blue! It made for deadly confusion on more than one early battlefield of the war.

Other units were even more gaily attired. The 6th Alabama Infantry joined the Confederate service in green uniforms, and wearing coonskin caps, while the 1st United States Sharpshooters also wore green. Men of the 79th New York "Highlanders" wore plaid pants, and came equipped even with kilts for formal occasions. Louisiana's Pelican Guard wore tri-corner hats and long, buttoned-back coats that made them look as if they had stepped out of time from the Revolution. The poor men of the 2nd New Hampshire arrived in gray coattee's with swallow tails more in keeping for butlers than soldiers, while their headgear looked like nothing so much as a German soldier's helmet from World War II.

But most resplendent – and from a practical point of view, ridiculous – were the zouaves. Such regiments patterned themselves after French Algerian units of the past decade, and their outfits were long on color, and short on practicality. Their

headgear told the whole story. The 114th Pennsylvania wore white cloth turbans. The 1st Louisiana Battalion wore red fezzes with braided tassels. Trousers were equally impractical, usually baggy pantaloons in bright red, white, or blue, with the Louisianians wearing blue and white stripes. As for their jackets, they were the most impractical of all. Some wore more or less regulation blouses, but most opted for tunics even shorter than a cavalryman's, gaudily covered with embroidered "frogging," and brass buttons – lots of buttons. One regiment's jacket had 22 buttons in either side, but no buttonholes! It was made so that it was impossible to button closed, in order not to obscure the equally gaudy shirt underneath.

Most of the zouave clothing was flimsy and impractical, and did not survive the war, as the majority of volunteers were eventually clothed in more practical regulation wear by 1865. Even so, when the soldiers in blue, gray, or whatever color, looked back years later upon their war years, one of the things they remembered with the most fondness and pride was the uniform in which they went off to risk their youth on the battlefield.

FACING PAGE: A posed photograph intended to appear as if the seated Zouave had just been wounded. Still, this 1862 image by Brady & Co. shows excellent details of the Zouave's uniform, including his white canvas puttees, the leather leggings above them, his baggy pantaloons, Zouave jacket, and close fitting turban-style fez.
ABOVE: The 114th Pennsylvania Infantry was a ceremonial Zouave outfit, attached to army headquarters and rarely in combat. Their full turbans were most unusual, though for the rest they wear a standard Zouave uniform much less extravagant than many.

CHAPTER TWO

EQUIPMENT

One of the unsung heroes of the Civil War, one who uncomplainingly sacrificed everything for the cause, was the cow. Armies literally marched on leather, and without the ubiquitous cowhide cavalrymen would have ridden bareback, soldiers would have walked on their bare feet, caps would have had no visors, fighting men no equipment for their rifles, nor belts to hold such equipment – and their trousers – up, and more. Blue and gray and all the colors of the rainbow may have been on the soldiers' backs, but they wore black or brown around their waists and on their feet.

The most important leather of all to a soldier lay between him and the ground. Boots and shoes were a far cry then from what they became in later years. Very often a pair did not differentiate between left and right foot at all, and the soldier simply wore thick enough socks to pad out the empty spaces. He did the same to make up for inadequacies in size, for boots and shoes came most often simply in two or three catch-all sizes. Regulations in the Union provided for boots for cavalrymen, and boots or shoes for the other branches, but infantrymen especially soon found that boots "were not agreeable on a long march," preferring "good, strong brogues or brogans, with broad bottoms and big flat heels." Of all the items of

FACING PAGE: The Civil War soldier paid little enough attention to regulations, and many even less attention to whatever they wore. This French caricature does not entirely overstate the condition of some soldiers, but more likely he would discard the greatcoat entirely, for the men found them too hot and too cumbersome. LEFT: Some vital pieces of the infantryman's equipment that he did not discard. The Sharps, whether in the infantry rifle version or the carbine shown here, was prized. But equally regarded was the blanket roll atop the leather or "rubberized" canvas knapsack. Everything the soldier owned and valued was inside that container or rolled up in the blanket. BELOW: Next in utility to the weapon were a soldier's shoes. Most were crudely made to standard patterns, often not differentiating between right and left feet, but they were more important even than the knapsack. Only folklore said that an army marched on its stomach. It was what was on the feet that controlled how far and how fast a soldier could move.

Civil War apparel that survive today, footwear is the rarest. The men simply wore them out too fast. For Confederates it was even worse. "Shoes are very scarce," wrote one during the war. "The men get pieces of raw hide from the butchers, and, after wrapping their feet up in old rags, sew the hide around them."

Next in importance to footwear was the soldier's belt. Actually, the well equipped soldier might wear two belts. One simply held up his trousers. The other he wore outside his tunic, and it was this two-inch wide length of blackened leather, his accoutrements belt, that carried much of what he needed to be a fighting man. A bewildering variety of buckles and belt plates held it together. In the Union the predominant one was a simple brass oval with the letters "US." The Confederates used much the same pattern, with a "CS," but literally scores of other types went to war – rectangles, circles, squares, stars – with an untold variation of devices, from eagles to state seals to patriotic mottoes, etched upon them.

The belt of a well-equipped infantryman would hold a small pouch with a leather flap for holding the percussion caps that fired his rifle, a sling from which hung the scabbard for his bayonet, and

FACING PAGE: An unidentified Virginia camp scene showing the soldiers' winter quarters log huts, some with tents stretched over the tops for roofs. Makeshift stools, tools, and other camp articles abound, most to be discarded when spring puts the men on the the move once more.
ABOVE: The governments were responsible for providing uniforms and equipment, and this depot of army clothing and equipage for the Union was erected in Washington, pouring forth an unending stream of cloth, leather, and more.

LEFT: Winslow Homer's tribute to the worn riding boots of a cavalryman, symbolic of the footgear of whole armies.

BELOW: Colonel C. H. T. Collis sits in his tent at Petersburg in 1864, surrounded by the paraphernalia of a headquarters tent in the Union Army.

RIGHT: A jumbled mix of the articles most common to the eyes of the average infantryman. The bleached canvas knapsack is more typical of the Confederate infantryman, while the tin canteen is Union standard issue. The leather cartridge book with its brass medallion could be from either side, as could the cloth-wrapped cannon scatter load beside it. The Schenkl shell lying on its side and the solid rifle bolt are probably Union in origin.

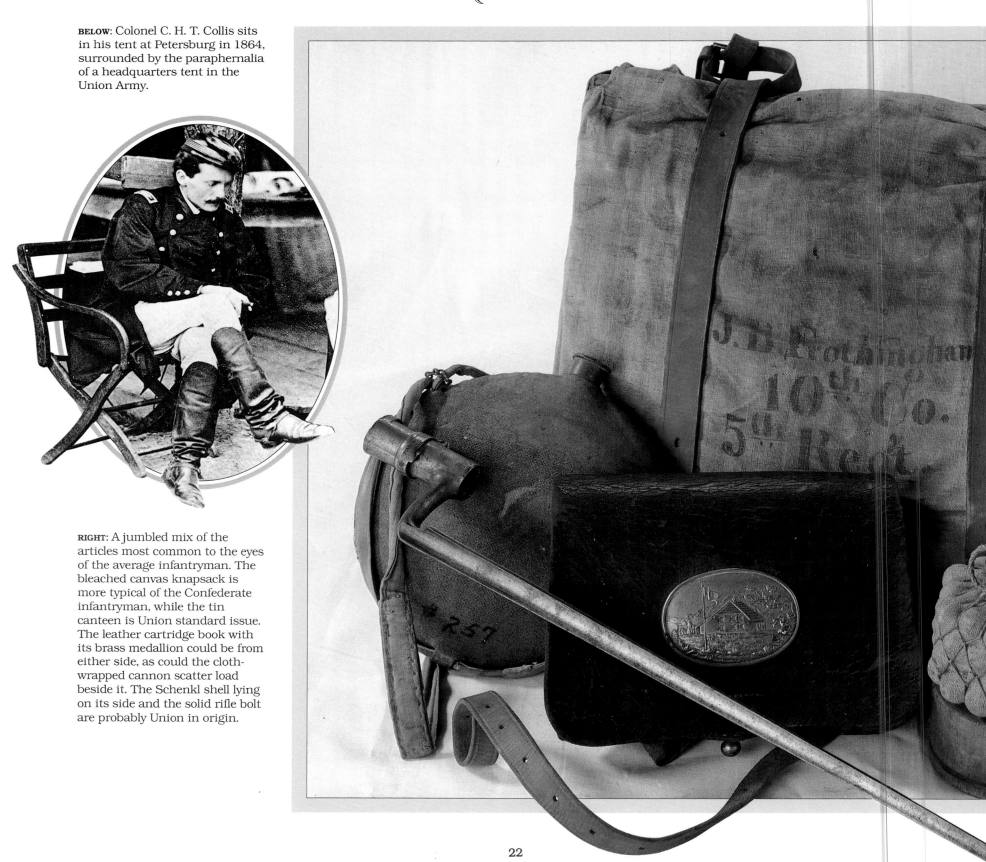

EQUIPMENT

perhaps his leather cartridge box. This last was a rectangular container, with an outer and inner flap, holding a tin compartment box in which sat the paper-wrapped cartridges for his rifle. On the front face of the cartridge box there was also a small pocket, with another flap, for carrying small tools for cleaning the rifle. If not worn on the waist belt, the cartridge box would be suspended from a cross belt worn over one shoulder and across the chest.

BOTTOM: A Federal-style canteen covered with canvas. The soldiers often abandoned them, for the water quickly acquired a stale taste and was not as cool as that from a fresh spring or stream.
BELOW: A variety of soldiers' shoes, showing both their construction and some of the efforts made to add to their life with reinforcing.

Not everything in the soldier's kit was leather, of course, though these goods are the ones that have most often survived. He was also issued a haversack, usually of canvas or oilcloth, which he wore slung over one shoulder by its strap, and in which he carried rations and other small personal items. Soldiers did not write admiringly of the "odorous haversack, which often stinks with its mixture of bacon, pork, salt junk, sugar, coffee, tea, desiccated vegetables, rice, bits of yesterday's dinner, and old scraps."

Regulations also called for a knapsack, again of canvas or oilcloth, to be worn on the back and held up by the arms being placed through leather straps like a modern backpack. Soldiers found it to be "an unwieldy burden," laden as it usually was with

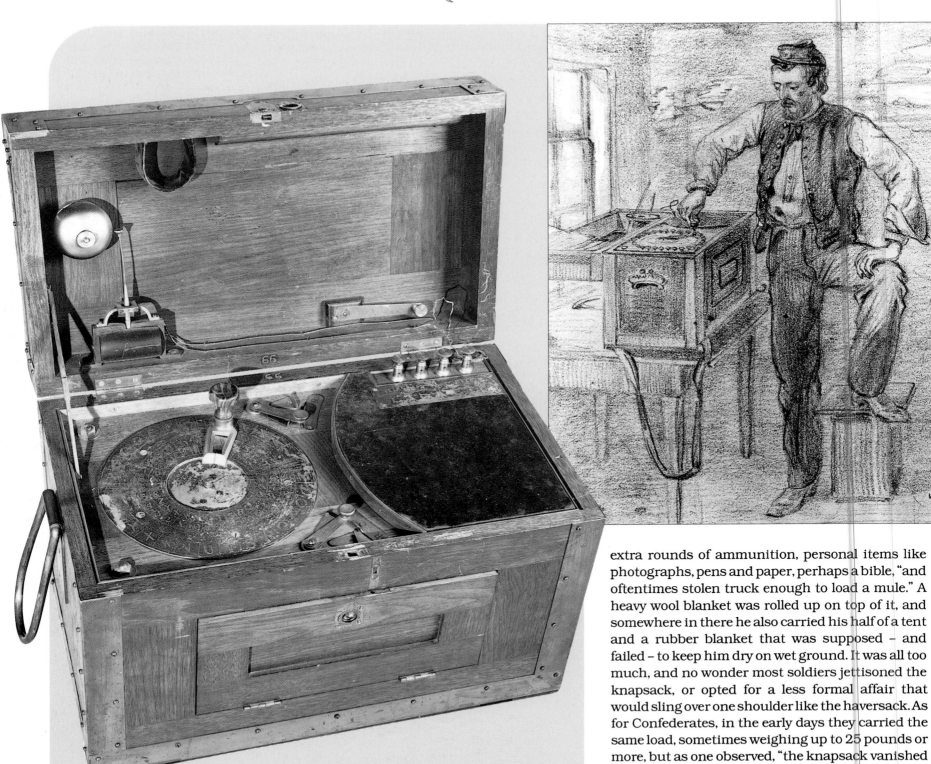

extra rounds of ammunition, personal items like photographs, pens and paper, perhaps a bible, "and oftentimes stolen truck enough to load a mule." A heavy wool blanket was rolled up on top of it, and somewhere in there he also carried his half of a tent and a rubber blanket that was supposed – and failed – to keep him dry on wet ground. It was all too much, and no wonder most soldiers jettisoned the knapsack, or opted for a less formal affair that would sling over one shoulder like the haversack. As for Confederates, in the early days they carried the same load, sometimes weighing up to 25 pounds or more, but as one observed, "the knapsack vanished early in the struggle." Instead of carrying a lot of spare clothing and gear, the Rebel preferred to wear all of his until it wore out, then replace it by

EQUIPMENT

FACING PAGE: Many soldiers had to deal with very specialized equipment in their daily endeavors. Much more complicated than a rifle or a saddle, the Beardslee Telegraph Machine was one such challenging apparatus, but fortunately only trained telegraphers had to deal with it. Artist A. R. Waud's pencil sketch (right) shows one such operator with the signal corps working his machine at Fredericksburg. To many soldiers, handling such items proved a constant challenge, and usually the machinery lost out.

ABOVE LEFT: For mounted men, cavalrymen and officers, a horse was one of the most vital pieces of "equipment," and none more so than General Grant's favorite mount, Cincinnati. ABOVE: For the foot soldier, the trappings he guarded most were in his knapsack, hence this Baxter's patent knapsack frame and harness.

capturing the enemy's. As a result, such Confederate gear was scarce at the outset, and very little of it survived at all.

Cavalrymen and artillerymen had their own specialized gear. For the mounted man, of course, his leather saddle was the most obvious. Saddles had been heavy, cumbersome things until 1859, when a new, lightweight saddle that was easy on rider and animal was adopted from a design by George B. McClellan, who would be a failure as a Union general. It predominated in the Yankee service, and Confederates tried to copy it as well, though most Rebel horsemen furnished their own saddles in whatever pattern they could acquire. Horsemen also wore high-topped boots, some reaching above the knee, though they were very clumsy for walking. Those armed with percussion pistols and carbines carried appropriate cartridge boxes on their belts,

and cap pouches. If they carried more modern weapons like the Spencer carbine, then special, leather-covered wooden cartridge boxes would hang from their saddle. An artilleryman, by contrast, would be expected to have an artillery fuse box of leather hanging from a belt, and perhaps a leather haversack for more fuses, lanyard, friction primers, and other paraphernalia needed for firing a cannon.

As with everything during the Civil War, the Union soldier of all branches generally came close to the ideal in equipment, while the poor Confederate rarely got all he was supposed to have, and more often had to provide for himself. As a result, genuine Rebel equipment artifacts were and are rare; a great deal of what Johnny Reb used was never official military issue in the first place, while much of the rest came to his hands by convenience, when he took it from dead or captured Yankees.

CHAPTER THREE

FLAGS AND INSIGNIA

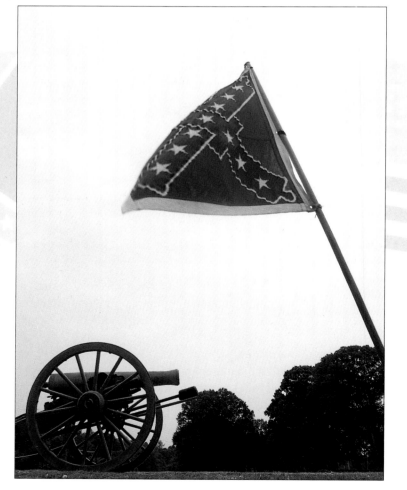

ABOVE: Men would follow their banners to their deaths, none more loyally than the soldiers of the Confederacy, for whom their flag was a symbol of their cause.

As perishable as his woolen uniforms and leather equipments might have been, the banners that the Civil War soldier followed into battle were even more fragile. Many were made of silk, hardly the most enduring of fabrics. Others were lovingly made from wedding dresses by wives who sent their husbands to war. Cotton composed the majority. But whatever their material, their fate was to be furled and unfurled repeatedly, to be subjected to all the elements from wind to rain and burning sun, and to be handled inordinately by adoring men. That alone would be enough to fray and fragment such materials. But then in battle the flag became the most sought-after prize of all, and hundreds of men literally died for their banners. Bullets, shot and shell, saber blades and bayonets, and the flames of combat, all flew around – and through – the flags in front of the regiments, so that by war's end many a fighting outfit's colors were nothing but a few shreds of tatters nailed to a staff.

Moreover, among Confederate regiments there was a special danger to their flags: the Johnny Reb's themselves. Scores – perhaps even hundreds – of Rebel regiments, faced with final surrender in 1865, chose to bury, burn, or otherwise destroy their beloved banners rather than yield them to the victors as spoils of war. Many more were cut into

On the flag:
M.CLELLAN CAVALRY 20.th N.Y.V.C

Col. A. B. Lord.

EXCELSIOR

The UNION must and shall be preserved.

dozens of tiny pieces, to give each surviving man a souvenir of his service to take home with him. Consequently, Confederate banners are the rarest of all.

As with everything else, there was no such thing as uniformity. However, a representative Union regiment would carry at least two flags at its front. One was the national colors, simply a 6-foot by 6-foot, 6-inch Stars and Stripes, with the name and number of the unit printed on the third red stripe from the bottom. There was also a regimental color, the same size, with a gold eagle appearing on a field of blue, and the regiment's name below. Many a Yankee outfit, however, also carried its particular state flag along with the other banners, and a few units that were privately raised and funded, like

ABOVE: Many of the banners were very ornate, like this regimental flag of the 20th New York Cavalry, the McClellan Cavalry. To carry such a banner into battle was a post of honor.

FACING PAGE: The color guard of the 118th New York Infantry, photographed in 1865 at war's end, demonstrating the rigors through which the flags and the men who carried them passed. The regimental flag is in tatters, while the national colors, its stripes showing at the bottom, carries embroidered on its folds the names of the battles it has come through. LEFT: James Walker's painting of the review of the colors of New England regiments offers an idea of the reverence felt for the flags.

BELOW: A ghostly banner with crossed cannon appears fluttering at left, marking artillery headquarters for a division.

some of the local militia outfits, had their own distinctive banner as well.

Among Confederates, as usual, there was even greater variety. For one thing, the national flag changed several times during the war. The first Confederate flag had a blue field in its corner, with a circle of stars representing each state, while the rest was pure white. That was soon changed by adding a red vertical stripe to the end, so that when the flag hung limp from a staff it did not show all white, looking like a sign of truce or surrender. Then came the 1st National Flag, with the same blue field, and three broad horizontal stripes, red top and bottom, and white in between, the so-called "Stars and Bars." But the most enduring symbol

ABOVE: This wartime woodcut of the Battle of Stones River on January 2, 1863 demonstrates the roles a flag could play in a fight. Confederates desperately give their lives trying to rally to protect it, while the attacking Federals lunge towards it as a focal point of their attack. Men won the Medal of Honor for capturing such battleflags.

was another banner entirely, the Battle Flag, a blue St. Andrew's cross on a red field, with thirteen stars spaced evenly on the arms of the cross. It was 4 feet by 4 feet when mass produced for presentation to Confederate infantry units (smaller for cavalry and artillery), and it is the banner that the men fought for most devotedly.

But Rebels carried a wonderful assortment of banners of their own devising into battle along with their various national flags. Many proclaimed bold mottoes, or the extravagant names of the unit, like the "Bartow Yankee Killers," the "Dixie Rangers," the "Racoon Roughs," and more. Some were huge, far too big for a man to carry aloft on a staff, especially in battle. Others were state flags, and

even private banners with nothing more than crayon crudely scrawled on a sheet. Ideally a regiment carried the national flag and the battle flag, but in practice they carried whatever they had.

Besides these major banners, Civil War soldiers also left behind special ones that denoted brigades, divisions, corps, and even armies, as well as the headquarters flags used by some generals. In the Union army most corps banners simply had the particular badge device of the corps – Maltese cross for the V Corps, star for the XII Corps, and more – with the division denoted by its color: red for the 1st division, white for the 2nd, and blue for the 3rd. Confederate corps and division flags were never formalized, but were usually stars on a red, white, or

blue field. Most Union, and some Confederate, artillery batteries had special guidons used to mark the battery's line in battle. It was usually either a small, swallow-tailed national banner, or a red triangular pennant with crossed cannon. Cavalry units carried similar guidons, only with crossed sabers.

While most flags were too fragile and saw too much hard service to survive, or to survive as much more than tatters, the individual identifying insignia that the men wore on their uniforms have proved more enduring, for oftentimes a soldier at the end of the war saved his insignia as a memento, while discarding a worn-out uniform.

The insignia for enlisted men was borrowed unchanged from the Old Army, and virtually the same North and South. The lowly private wore none at all. With his first promotion he got a single chevron, worn midway down both sleeves, point facing downward. The corporal got a second stripe, and the sergeant a third. Within the upper NCO ranks there were gradations. First corporals and first sergeants wore a diamond inside the angle of their top chevron. A sergeant major wore "rockers," semi-circular stripes arching above and connecting the ends of his chevrons. A commissary sergeant had a single horizontal stripe connecting the uppermost of his chevrons, and sometimes a corporal in the same service would show that extra

LEFT: Insignia varied wildly, especially in the South, where many men provided their own uniforms. This sergeant's coatee is covered with mysterious, non-regulation insignia. TOP: Shepherd G. Pryor of the 12th Georgia shows the lace on his sleeve denoting an officer – usually. ABOVE: Company B of the 125th Ohio shows a hodge-podge of uniform styles and enlisted men's insignia.

ABOVE LEFT: Even generals, or more likely, especially generals, were not immune to the temptation to vary from regulations in uniform. Major General David G. Birney wears shoulder straps that look almost homemade, and a collar that appears to be velvet. ABOVE RIGHT: Major General Nathaniel P. Banks wears the proper shoulder straps, but has had a pocket inserted on his tunic and sports a bow tie at his collar.

stripe. Ideally, the stripes were to match the color of the branch of service – blue for infantry, and so on – yet much of the time, even in the Union, individual regiments varied widely.

The variation was even greater in the Confederacy, where often as not an NCO's recognition of status simply depended upon his men knowing who he was. Insignias were in short supply, like everything else. Worse, many units simply made up their own. One cavalry outfit had the silhouette of a mounted rider on each sleeve. Other units showed rank by arrangements of buttons on the cuffs. Even today the actual rank of

some of the men who peer out at us from the old photographs can only be guessed, and it was just as confusing for their fellow soldiers in other units.

Confederate insignia among officers was also confusing to a degree. It was worn on the collar, in gold braid. One horizontal stripe for a second lieutenant, two for a first lieutenant, and three for a captain. Then they changed to stars: one for a major, two for a lieutenant colonel, three for a colonel. However, even though the Confederate Army had four grades of general – brigadier, major, lieutenant, and full general – all wore precisely the same insignia of three stars surrounded by a wreath.

ABOVE: A non-commissioned officers' mess of Company D, 93d New York Infantry, in August 1863. The chevrons on their sleeves tell the story of their rank: sergeants, corporals and, third from right, a sergeant with dark red or blue stripes instead of yellow. **FAR LEFT:** Two officers of the 12th United States Infantry. Their shoulder straps show them to be a captain at right, and a first lieutenant at left, and infantry is indicated by the bugles on their caps, though the seated officer has the yellow straps usually reserved for cavalrymen. Even the regulars, it seems, took liberties with their outfits.

LEFT: Brigadier General Isaac I. Stevens shows what the natty Federal commander should look like, down to his sash and sword knot, and knee-length leather boots.

RIGHT: A group of officers at rest in winter quarters, probably in Virginia. Their cap bugles show them to be infantry, but beyond that they cannot be identified. The double row of buttons on the man seated far right does suggest that he is a major or lieutenant colonel, even a colonel perhaps, but nothing more is revealed.
BELOW: A family group of Confederates, all serving in the same regiment, the 22d Georgia Infantry. All six are brothers named Jones. In the back row, left to right, are the regimental chaplain, a lieutenant, and a corporal. In the front row, left to right, are the surgeon, Colonel R. H. Jones, and a captain. Clearly for these men the war was a family affair.

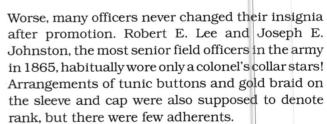

Worse, many officers never changed their insignia after promotion. Robert E. Lee and Joseph E. Johnston, the most senior field officers in the army in 1865, habitually wore only a colonel's collar stars! Arrangements of tunic buttons and gold braid on the sleeve and cap were also supposed to denote rank, but there were few adherents.

In the Union things were much more uniform, and virtually the same as today. Insignia appeared on straps affixed to each shoulder. An empty strap, surrounded by gold bullion, denoted a second lieutenant. A first lieutenant got a bar at each end. A captain got two bars at each end. A major had to oak leaves in gold. A lieutenant colonel two oak leaves in silver. A colonel an eagle in silver. The grades of general, brigadier and major, were shown respectively by one and two stars. Only Grant held the higher ranks of lieutenant general – three stars – and full general – four stars.

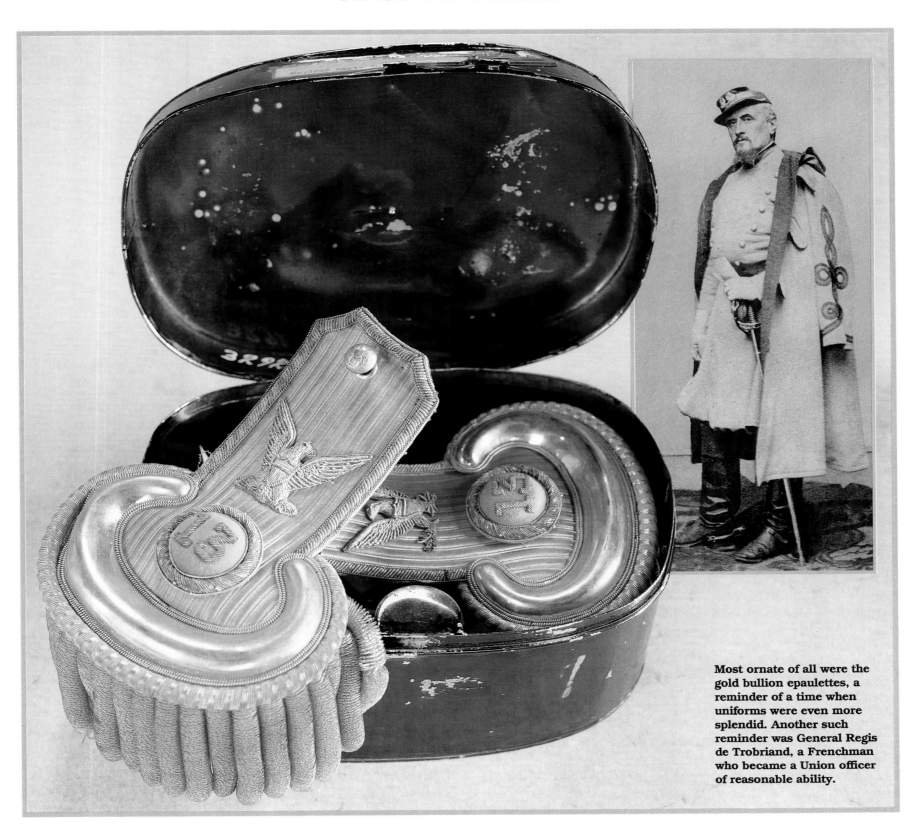

Most ornate of all were the gold bullion epaulettes, a reminder of a time when uniforms were even more splendid. Another such reminder was General Regis de Trobriand, a Frenchman who became a Union officer of reasonable ability.

CHAPTER FOUR

CAMP EQUIPMENT

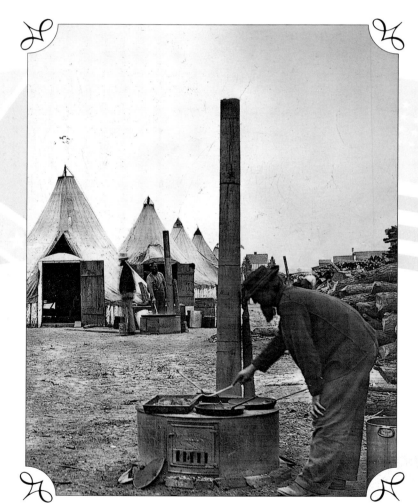

W hile the enlisted men learned to recognize the officers' insignia, they rarely learned to respect it. The average private soldier had far more regard – and concern – for the everyday things that surrounded him, and with which he tried as he could to make the hard ground his home.

Most important of all, especially in the bad weather that often dogged him, was his shelter. At first many regiments were equipped with what were called "wall" tents, straight-sided canvas rectangles with peaked canvas roofs, that looked just like a house in shape. But they were cumbersome, and soon abandoned in favor of the Sibley tent. It looked

ABOVE: The soldier's mind was always on his stomach, and the camp stove was a coveted article.
FACING PAGE: The 5th Vermont Infantry on parade in 1862.

exactly like an Indian teepee and was generally popular, though uncomfortable when filled with up to twenty coughing, snoring, men. Some regiments used a simple wedge tent, like those of latter-day Boy Scouts, but by late in the war most soldiers were sleeping in what they called "dog tents." Two soldiers each carried a "fly" – one half of the tent. At night they buttoned their halves together, slung them over a makeshift ridgepole, and staked the ends to the ground.

Inside those tents, or the more formal and semi-permanent huts the men built for winter quarters, comfort depended upon many things. Well-equipped regiments had stoves, usually nothing more than

RIGHT: A typical winter quarters' scene in the Union army, with men chopping wood, cutting meat, cooking, bringing water from a spring, and more. It was almost all makeshift, like the "corduroy" street in front of their huts to keep out the winter mud.
BELOW: Soldiers were issued, or bought, a variety of eating utensils, but the spoon-fork or spoon-knife combination was one of the commonest. His government gave him a canteen, but he likely threw it away as being too cumbersome, or too leaky, to be practical. He much preferred the simple tin cup, while his tin plate he carried stuffed into his knapsack.

small iron cones with stovepipes, that provided heat. Some actually had miniature kitchen "ranges" which soldiers could use for cooking, as well as keeping warm. To keep himself dry – or to try to – the soldier slept on a "rubber blanket," really just a wool army issue blanket laid over a rubber-impregnated canvas.

Even more important to Reb and Yank than his sleeping gear was what he used for cooking and eating. At the start of the war many regiments, North and South, marched off with large camp chests for each "mess," or group of tent mates. Frying pans and skillets, coffee boiler, buckets for lard and butter, boxes for coffee, salt, sugar, flour, corn meal, and so on; cutlery, plates, cups, and more filled these unwieldy chests, and they were soon discarded. "The camp-chest soon vanished," wrote one veteran. "One skillet and a couple of frying pans, a bag of flour or meal, another bag of salt, sugar and coffee," he said, "served the purpose as well." The skillets were of iron, and almost everything else of tin or, occasionally, pewter, with wooden or bone handles. By the end of the war the men had learned to use only as much as they could carry with them. Many even discarded their canteens, preferring to carry a tin cup and take advantage of streams and wells while on the march. In addition, they could use the cup to heat their coffee over a fire. Mess

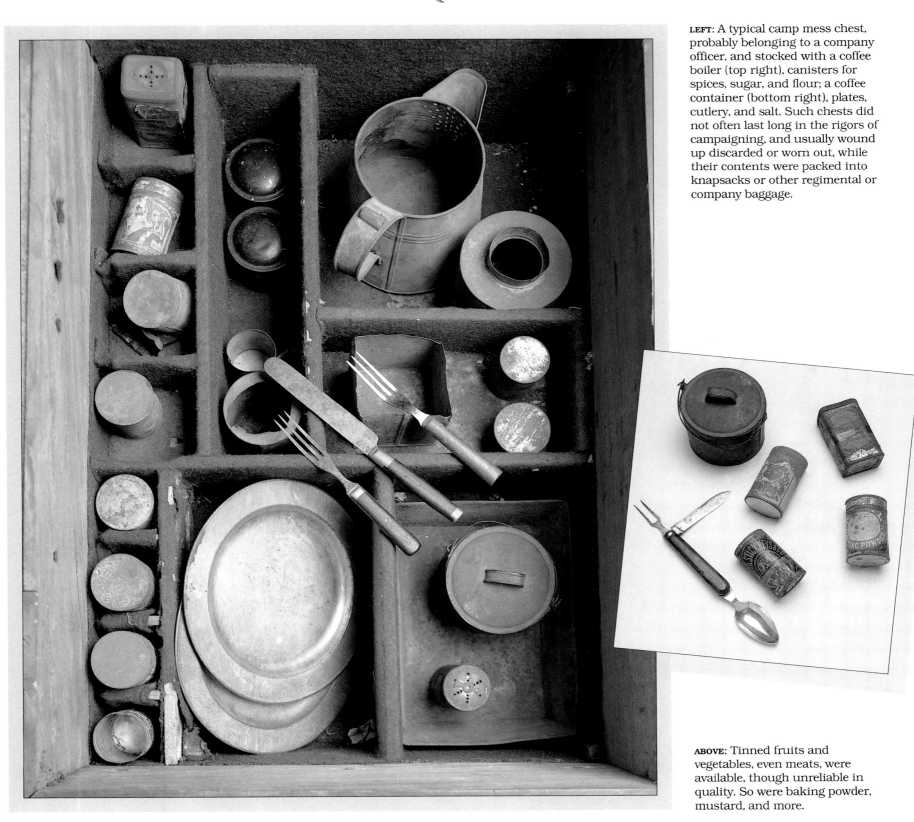

LEFT: A typical camp mess chest, probably belonging to a company officer, and stocked with a coffee boiler (top right), canisters for spices, sugar, and flour; a coffee container (bottom right), plates, cutlery, and salt. Such chests did not often last long in the rigors of campaigning, and usually wound up discarded or worn out, while their contents were packed into knapsacks or other regimental or company baggage.

ABOVE: Tinned fruits and vegetables, even meats, were available, though unreliable in quality. So were baking powder, mustard, and more.

RIGHT: A soldier, probably from the 49th New York, sits for a posed meal in front of the camera. His coffee cup is in one hand, a piece of hardtack in the other, while before him are a coffee boiler, a plate with more hardtack and potatoes, and a skillet with what appears to be either a chunk of bread or a portion of meat.

ABOVE: The decidedly-luxurious tent of an officer shows the difference between his living quarters and those of the enlisted man. He has a cot with pillow and blanket, a folding camp chair, a table and even a tablecloth. His sabers hang over his head, and a knitted shawl hangs beneath his kepi. There is even what appears to be a military print adorning the wall, while a Bible, other books and current magazines clutter the table, along with scissors and sewing kit, a cased photograph of some loved one, and a candlestick.

equipment was always prized, and often the object of "raids" by one regiment on another. Thus a Kentucky outfit in the Confederate Army of Tennessee became known by their sobriquet "Coffee Boiler Rangers."

Beyond what he cooked with, the soldier carried a number of other domestic items. One was his "housewife," literally a sewing kit for mending his uniform. None were actually issued by the armies, so every man's was highly individual, sometimes sent from home by a wife or mother, or else made by the soldier himself. Some even embroidered patriotic mottoes on the little cloth bags or rolls that carried needle, thread, buttons, yarn, and bits of wool or cotton for patching. "My true love is Dixie," one Reb inscribed on his kit.

ABOVE: In the late spring of 1862 a number of servants working for a wealthy officer perform some of the routine camp chores, polishing his saber and scabbard, washing clothing in a wooden tub, pretending to cook in a skillet over a fire that is not burning! LEFT: Colonel Henry Hoffman of the 230th New York sits in the comfort of his tent with bed, table, chairs, even a floor; comforts most could only dream of in the field.

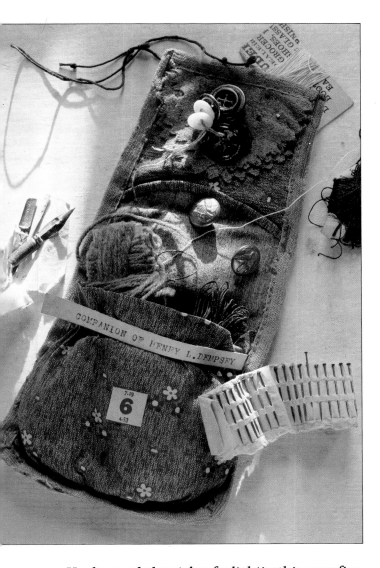

He also needed matches for lighting his campfire or his pipe, and more or less "modern" striking matches were widely manufactured at the time. Most often they were slender sheets of soft pine, nearly scored through so that a match was easily broken off the pack, and with the tips covered with the igniting compound. Some were called "loco-foco's," a nickname briefly given to pre-war Democrats when they illuminated a convention by striking hundreds of matches.

Many a soldier did not bother to shave in an era of elaborate whiskers, but those who did carried straight razors, pocket mirrors, and bone or hard rubber combs. The toothbrush was virtually unknown in the armies.

FACING PAGE: A recreation of a makeshift indoor bivouac, strewn with blankets, cups, and the kind of commercially-available cooking utensils that sutlers sold to soldiers. **TOP LEFT:** The "soldier's companion" of Private Henry Dempsey is unusually complete, with yarns for darning, finer threads for sewing on patches, buttons, a good number of pins, and even some nibs for his pen. **TOP RIGHT:** The tent of Lieutenant J. B. Neill of the 153d New York is certainly well appointed and comfortable, with even a traveling trunk, washing pans, and a shelf for books. **LEFT:** Inside the Stone House at Manassas, a hospital during the two battles that raged there, a host of paraphernalia including cups, a litter, and more items familiar to all soldiers can be seen.

CHAPTER FIVE

ENTERTAINMENTS

ABOVE: Soldier fun involved a variety of games, like this climb for prizes. FACING PAGE: Music, cards and gambling, and drink were much the preferred pastimes.

Crammed as Yank and Reb knapsacks were with just the necessities of soldier life, still they usually managed to find room for at least a few things to brighten the monotony of camp life and the march. Years later, as old men, they would often recall these simple pleasures most fondly of all the experiences of their war.

There was hardly a mess that did not have at least one pipe smoker. Many were commercially manufactured briars, but many more the soldiers simply made themselves. They used clay, tree knots, soapstone, and more, to fashion highly individualistic items, some approaching works of art. Beautiful red soapstone

pipes with "Chickamauga" or "Stones River," puffed in Yankee mouths all across Georgia. Cigars and cheroots were also highly in demand, and here at least, Johnny Reb had the best of it. Indeed, when soldiers of opposing sides met informally – and against regulations – between the lines, Confederates most often traded abundantly available Southern tobacco in return for good Yankee coffee.

Few regarded smoking as a vice, but another pastime often associated with it, drinking, left a host of artifacts to testify to its popularity in the armies. Mostly they drank a rye whiskey that was locally distilled and bottled in whatever was handy,

44

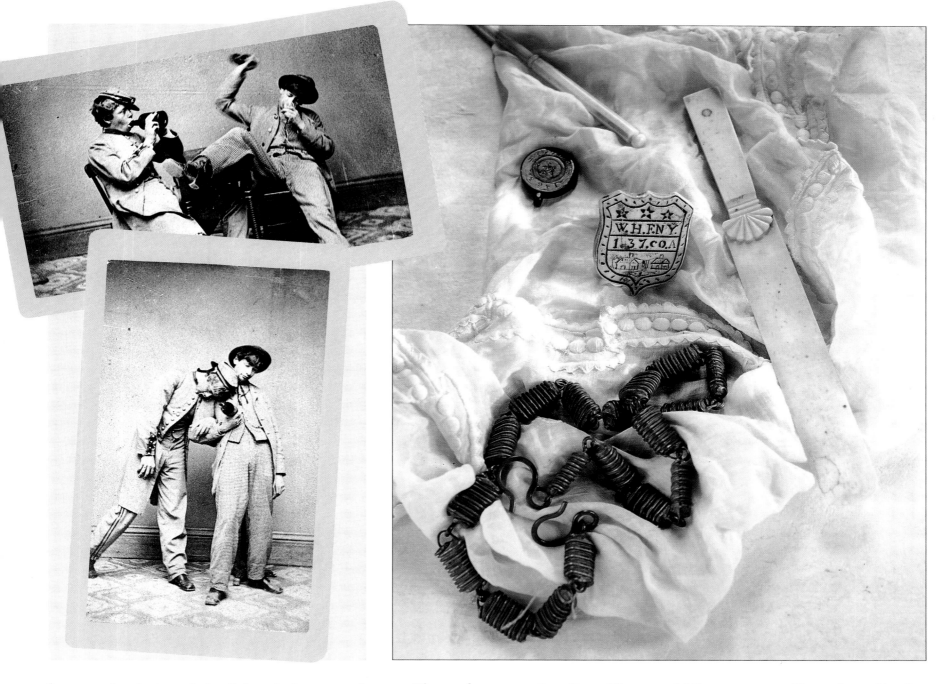

from wooden kegs and demijohns to brown and green glass bottles. Beer and porter were also popular. Ironically, what most often survives to testify to their alcohol consumption are the empty patent medicine bottles with which they treated their ailments. Most such "remedies" were nothing more than herbal extracts with little or no healing property, mixed with a liberal solution of alcohol.

Those of a more sober disposition spent idle hours reading – if they knew how. Both North and South enjoyed a flourishing press before the war, and even in the Confederacy publishing continued to be productive almost until the end. Illustrated newspapers were especially popular. *Harper's Weekly Illustrated Newspaper* and *Frank Leslie's Illustrated Newspaper*, along with the *New York*

FACING PAGE: Those who could write kept diaries. Those who could get tobacco smoked. ABOVE: Many spent idle hours making items such as badges, fans, even pens, from metal, ivory or bone, or fashioning chains and necklaces. LEFT: Drinking was so common that it was the subject of jest and play-acting.

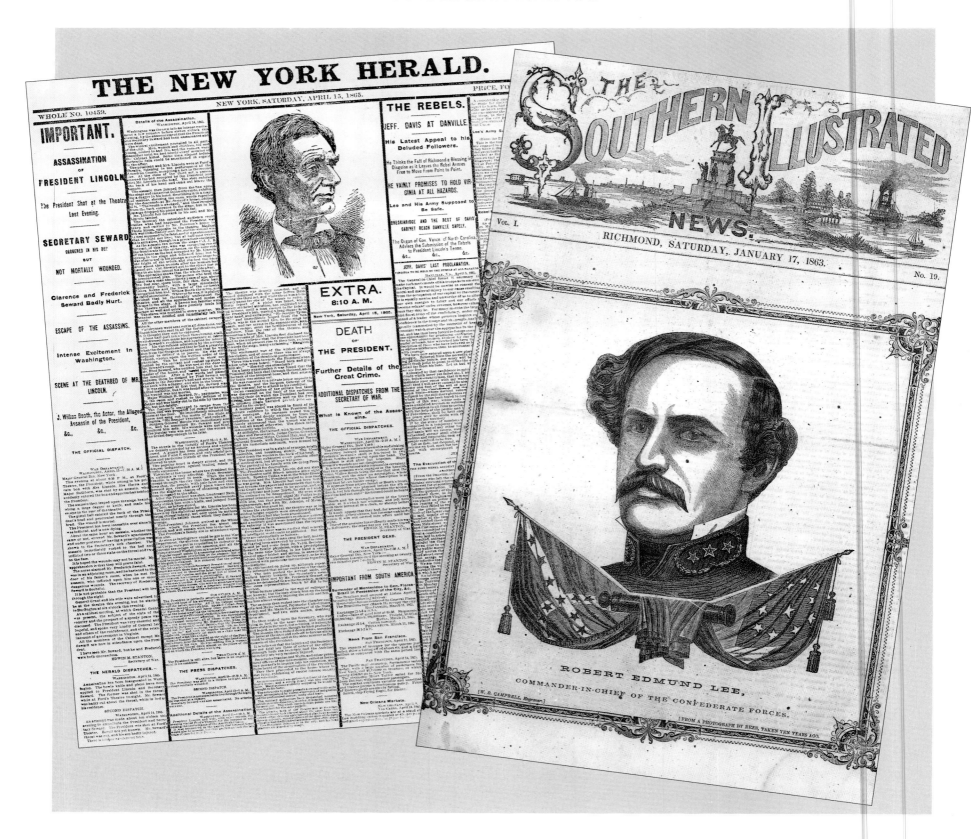

Illustrated News, brought Yankees weekly accounts of world and national affairs, war news especially, and even serializations of maudlin romantic novels. The illustrations were crude woodcuts based upon sketches sent in by battlefield artists traveling with the armies. In Richmond the *Southern Illustrated News* also operated for a time in 1861-1862.

Conventional newspapers were always in demand, and often traded across the lines with the tobacco and coffee. When these were not available, some regiments published sheets of their own, usually on captured presses. Confederate John Hunt Morgan's celebrated cavalry published a paper called *The Vedette* for a time, and many a Yankee outfit issued its own "regimental" broadside.

Equally as popular in the knapsacks of the literate were current novels, especially Walter Scott and Charles Dickens. Now and again Shakespeare could be found, but the Bible was by far the most prevalent book, tens of thousands being issued to the soldiers by benevolent associations like the U.S. Christian Commission and the Southern Relief Society.

FACING PAGE: Reading material was very important to all, literate or not. Illustrated newspapers flourished in the North, and one was published briefly in the South as well. **ABOVE AND RIGHT:** News vendors visited both armies, peddling newspapers, magazines, even books, to a hungry audience.

MAIN PICTURE: **Nothing was more important to the boys in the field than word from home. Both armies operated mail services, such as this Union II Corps mail wagon, the mail bag before it bulging with letters. So prized was mail that men who could not write dictated letters to friends who could.**

FACING PAGE, INSET TOP: **The patriotic fervor of the war years was carried over into everything, even the stationery and envelopes used by soldiers and civilians. These "patriotics" proclaim devotion to the Union and faith in the justice of its cause.** INSET BOTTOM: **A Yankee field post office.**

BELOW: Music was a vital entertainment for all, and many an outfit had its informal players, like this band from an Ohio regiment, in addition to the formal regimental bands.
BOTTOM: The presses churned out sheet music, often maudlin, for soldier consumption.

Other printed and published works were less elevated. "Spirited and Spicy" French photographs circulated widely, showing scantily clad models in classical poses. Though hardly pornographic, nevertheless they were considered scandalous in their day, and so were the penny and dime novels, sometimes illustrated with crude woodcuts, that pandered to a lonely soldier's daydreams.

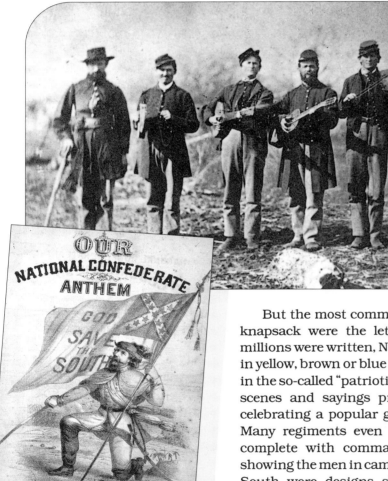

But the most common reading material in his knapsack were the letters from home. Literally millions were written, North and South. They came in yellow, brown or blue tissue envelopes, and often in the so-called "patriotic" envelopes with elaborate scenes and sayings printed on front and flap, celebrating a popular general or a recent victory. Many regiments even had their own envelopes, complete with commander's profile and a cut showing the men in camp. Especially popular in the South were designs showing variations of the Confederate flags, or cartoons depicting Lincoln as a baboon or a leering would-be rapist.

Almost as colorful were the stamps that paid for their delivery. Most of those in the Union were red, depicting Washington on a two cent denomination. In the Confederacy stamps appeared in five, ten, and twenty cent varieties, in colors ranging from a milky blue, to green, to rust, and even orange, most of them carrying portraits of Jefferson Davis.

RIGHT: They were rugged men in a rough era, and their fun often turned to the barbaric, such as cockfights like this one being staged in South Carolina.

FACING PAGE: Reminders of home helped fill a soldier's lonely hours. Most carried with them photographs, like these cased ambrotypes, of parents, sweethearts or wives. RIGHT: More refined pastimes included dominoes, checkers, and even chess now and then. BELOW: for soldiers inclined towards the decorative arts, such simple camp items as spoons offered a medium for expression, and for killing time. BOTTOM: The regimental band of the 26th North Carolina did its best to entertain the men when they could not entertain themselves.

Games, too, offered a lot of diversion. Both Northern and Southern manufacturers produced playing cards for the soldiers, often with patriotic or military figures replacing the usual sports and face cards. Portable chess and checkers sets commonly appeared in the tent, and even more homemade varieties nestled in the knapsacks. So did dominoes and cribbage boards, and the ubiquitous dice.

Meanwhile, as the card and dice games carried on, men disinclined – or too broke – to gamble, played their flutes and guitars and banjos. Every regiment had at least one man proficient with a country fiddle, and most saw such musicians group together – often with the official regimental drummer and bugler – to perform as a band. They were almost all instruments brought from home, except for the brass bugles and the brightly-colored drums issued by the armies. Some were even homemade from discarded bread boxes and cooking pots, but they all served their purpose to relieve in some way the tedium of the soldier's life.

CHAPTER SIX

BATTLEFIELD ARTIFACTS

ABOVE: Anything from a battlefield like Atlanta could become a treasured artifact.
FACING PAGE: Soldiers, and later relic hunters, combed fields like this at Kingston, Georgia.

When the war finally came to an end, the men in blue and gray who were still living, and still in the armies, took their uniforms, their camp equipment, sometimes even their weapons, back home with them. In time, most such mementoes were lost, discarded, or simply disintegrated. Some items they fortunately gave to museums, where they could be preserved for future generations to look at and appreciate. Others passed into the hands of a growing army of collectors, for whom acquiring Civil War memorabilia became a passion, as it remains today.

Yet there was a whole different class of artifacts that never went back home, that stayed where the men lived and fought and died. Untold tons of material, from buttons to bullets to belt buckles and more, fell or was dropped during the war. If not found right away, it disappeared in spring grass or under fallen leaves, and within a few years the natural churning action of the topsoil of the South in the changing of the seasons, cultivation, and the rooting of animals, saw much of this settle several inches beneath the surface. There it waited.

In fact, the first battlefield artifacts were being found as soon as the armies left. At Gettysburg a member of a local family spent days walking around the massive battlefield picking up objects left behind

RIGHT: Battlefield artifacts rarely if ever looked as fine as the pieces in this grouping, especially if they sat on the field for long after the fight. But these were all used on the battlefields, and are much treasured and sought after, the more so since they are Confederate in origin, and thus rarer. Rarest of all is the battleflag, in near perfect condition. Rare, too, is the C.S.A. belt plate, and even more hard to find is the two-piece round buckle with belt. The top saber is almost homemade, while the other is government issue, as is the kepi, but the knife definitely came from home. The battered and repaired pistol was almost a museum piece when the war was fought.

by the retreating Confederates and pursuing Federals. Hundreds of guns of every description were there to be found, along with overcoats, blankets, tents, stoves, sabers, saddles, artillery shells, caisson – virtually everything that moved with an army and could be left behind. The collection thus begun became in time the largest private collection of Civil War artifacts in existence, and fills a huge museum in the visitors' Center at the Gettysburg National Battlefield Park today. Similar, though much smaller, museums are dotted elsewhere around the United States, displaying these so-called battlefield "pick-ups."

FAR LEFT: Wartime maps were incomplete and wildly inaccurate, but still in demand, and this printed plan of Sharpsburg, Maryland, was of much interest to people in the North after Lee suffered his first major defeat there in the Battle of Antietam in September 1862.

Not surprisingly, the most numerous battlefield artefact of all is the bullet. But then it is not just *the* bullet. In fact, there are examples of more than a hundred different types of bullets. Most prevalent are the .58 caliber cylindroconoidal Minie "balls" used in both the Springfield and Enfield rifles, the two predominant infantry weapons of the war. Tens of millions were fired, and most hit nothing but the ground and the trees. They are easily identified by their hollow bases and pointed noses. The molds used to make Union bullets had three parallel rings around the base; for some reason most Confederate molds only had two rings, thus allowing an easy means of identification.

ABOVE: A modern view of the Cornfield at Antietam, where some of the bloodiest fighting of the war's bloodiest day took place. These fields were literally sown with lead, so much so that more than a century later bullets and shell fragments are still coming out of the ground every spring after the rains and the plowing.

Many other varieties also come out of the ground. Some bullets did not have the hollow bases, the so-called picket bullets. Other had slight "wings" for gripping the grooves in a rifle barrel. Very rare are the Jacobs' rifle exploding bullet with a pin in the nose. There might also be spent rounds from Burnside carbines, with their distinctive Ottoman's hat shape, or any of scores of other varieties.

Round balls, buck shot, iron grape shot, and iron balls an inch across used in artillery scatter loads, can also be found, along with fragments of exploding shells. Now and then a cannon solid shot or bolt comes to light.

LEFT: George N. Barnard's 1865 view of Confederate works surrounding Atlanta illustrates two kinds of artifacts much prized. Certainly the rifles, canteens and other equipment are highly desired today. But so are vintage photographs, especially from masters like Barnard, Alexander Gardner, Timothy O'Sullivan, and others.

Very few actual weapons are still to be found on the battlefields, though they kept appearing from time to time well into this century, usually found where they had dropped into rock crevices or creek beds. Still, they do occasionally turn up. Almost without exception, all wooden grips and stocks will have disintegrated, and the iron parts of the gun

ABOVE: Even the sea floor is yielding artifacts from the past, like this lantern base from the wreck of the Yankee ironclad USS *Monitor*, now at the bottom of the Atlantic.

RIGHT: Another Gardner image of Rebel works around Atlanta. When the armies passed, they left much behind. BELOW: Living artifacts are the battlefields themselves, many now preserved as parks.

FACING PAGE: Many simple reminders of the life the soldiers led have been left behind, including testimony to their occasional unruliness such as handcuffs and a key, or the pocket knife that was almost every soldier's companion.

will be heavily encrusted with rust. If a revolver is found, perish the thought of getting the cylinder to turn again. Bayonets and sabers will be heavily pitted, and may even have rusted through in places.

The one metal that survives best of all – almost perfectly, in fact – is brass, which means that belt plates and buckles, ornamental harness, insignia and buttons will all come out of the ground nearly as good as when new, only green with tarnish. Thus belt plates have become among the most prized of all battlefield pick ups. By contrast, fabric and leather have the least survivability, and will come to light again as little more than fragile fragments. As a result, such things as harness, saddlery, boots and shoes, belts and cartridge boxes, survive in no better condition than things wooden.

Yet an amazing variety of other items somehow seems to survive. Bottles still emerge intact, complete with their contents, though quite undrinkable. Even paper goods like newspapers and books sometimes, under some conditions, remain partially intact. Photographs on metal plates have come from the ground and had their images restored. And loaded shells, it should be added, are frequently found, and their powder charges, once dried out,

are just as explosive today as more than a century ago, and must only be handled by experts.

Indeed, so much remains in the ground that a veritable army of hunters armed with metal detectors today roams the former campsites and battlefields of the Civil War. Unfortunately, some do not honor the prohibitions against doing so on National Park and state park sites, and park officials have to remain ever-vigilant to prevent their grounds from being despoiled, and stiff fines and jail penalties can be, and are, imposed.

It is a measure of the lasting hold that the Civil War has upon Americans that the physical remains of the conflict are still so cherished today, so sought after. Thousands of home offices, libraries, and sitting rooms have the old saber or Springfield over the fireplace. Innumerable Americans keep an old bullet sitting as a curio on the desk, or use a shell fragment as a paperweight. A few even still use the belt plates that held up trousers of the 1860s, for the same purpose in the 1990s. Such usages may seem mundane, even trivial, yet they symbolize the living link that still binds Americans of our time to an era from which they could not escape even if they wished to.

CREDITS TO ILLUSTRATIONS
The publishers wish to thank the following individuals and organisations for granting permission to
reproduce the illustrations used in this book:

The Bettmann Archive; The Library of Congress, Washington, D.C.;
Washington Light Infantry, Chrleston, South Carolina; Terence P. O'Leary, Gladwyne, Pennsylvania;
The National Archives, Washington, D.C.; South Carolina Historical Society;
U.S. Army Military History Institute, Carlisle, Pennsylvania;
The New York Historical Society, New York City; Michael J. McAfee, West Point Library;
University of Georgia, Athens, Georgia; Minnesota Historical Society, St. Paul, Minnesota;
Civil War Library and Museum, Philadelphia, Pennsylvania; Mrs. Lucy Mulcahy, Atlanta, Georgia;
Lloyd Ostendorf, Dayton, Ohio; Dale S. Snair, Richmond, Virginia; T. Scott Sanders;
Moravian Music Foundation, Inc., North Carolina;
Georgia Department of Archives and History, Atlanta, Georgia;

ACKNOWLEDGMENT
The publishers wish to thank the New York State Division of Military and Naval Affairs, and the New York
State Military Heritage Museum for granting permission to photograph items from their collections.

ABOVE: The Blue and Gray never missed a chance to
relax, men and officers alike, and General Robert O.
Tyler, standing second from right, and his staff are no
different, though their sabers are ever present.